Sons of Achilles

Sons
of
Achilles

Nabila Lovelace

 YESYES BOOKS *Portland*

ISBN 978-1-936919-51-2

PRINTED IN THE UNITED STATES OF AMERICA

PUBLISHED BY YESYES BOOKS
1614 NE ALBERTA ST
PORTLAND, OR 97211
YESYESBOOKS.COM

KMA SULLIVAN, PUBLISHER
JOANN BALINGIT, ASSISTANT EDITOR
STEVIE EDWARDS, SENIOR EDITOR, BOOK DEVELOPMENT
ALBAN FISCHER, GRAPHIC DESIGNER
COLE HILDEBRAND, SENIOR EDITOR OF OPERATIONS
JILL KOLONGOWSKI, MANAGING EDITOR
BEYZA OZER, DEPUTY DIRECTOR OF SOCIAL MEDIA
AMBER RAMBHAROSE, CREATIVE DIRECTOR OF SOCIAL MEDIA
CARLY SCHWEPPE, ASSISTANT EDITOR, *VINYL*
PHILLIP B. WILLIAMS, COEDITOR IN CHIEF, *VINYL*
AMIE ZIMMERMAN, EVENTS COORDINATOR
HARI ZIYAD, ASSISTANT EDITOR, *VINYL*

Since I am what I am, how was I made?

—DEREK WALCOTT

There's a war goin' on outside no man is safe from.

—PRODIGY

Contents

The Preamble / 1

Sons of Achilles / 3

After the Funeral / 4

For Songs & Contests / 6

"They May Become Wise." / 7

Return to Sender / 8

Roy Wilkins Recreational Center / 9

For Songs & Contests / 10

Ed / 11

Moses II: The Lunchroom / 12

Repurposing a Funeral / 13

Exorcism / 14

Practice / 15

Let Me Tell You a Thing / 16

Veterans Memorial Drive / 17

The "S" in *I Loves You, Porgy* / 19

Cyclops Girl Is a Good Host / 20

Letter to the Choking / 21

Mr. & Me / 23

Roan Beauty & Charger / 24

Sharing Cake / 25

Finally, Weep Freely / 27

Don't Pretty Me / 29

Black Peter / 30

Hourglass / 31

When Your Vice Is a Man / 33

Roll Tide / 34

For the Days That Are Today / 36

Ruff Ryders Anthem / 38

For Songs & Contests / 39

"I Turned Myself Into Myself & Was Jesus" / 41

Citizenship / 42

Still, I Don't Love My Father / 44

Ugly / 46
On Knowing / 49

Untitled / 53

Notes / 57
Acknowledgments & Gratitude / 59

Sons of Achilles

The Preamble

When it wasn't profitable to bury
us you didn't & that's the story
                of the ground. Now
arising, check her fist
upside the cement.
What a light. Bring
that retribution here mama/ grandmama
      mama's mama's mama. Rose
herself out the Wall
Street bull, w/ all
our cousins to get
what you owe. She
a pretty cuticle. Cotton
all in the nail. Maggots
teeming eyelids, back
from the dead.

Arm your blood.
Forgo mine

& I've citizened
the zombie body.

Next
                —Poof!

Check the oven
for your head.

Sons of Achilles

If I think like the boy I take into me, then I know why
the blood appears. I am an apprentice in a city named,
Kiss The Hands Who Kill

& Achilles is the father. His sons crawl out war
with fully loaded hands. I meet Achilles & the streetlights

hush. Bootleg Jordans grant a tongue for my speechless. Praise
the bootlegger.

//

Outside, the streetlights bend to lend
a shine. The block is hot & the boys

keep coming. I cannot catalogue a thing

he didn't bear. Even the grass grows
his progeny.

//

Achilles & his sons.   Achilles is his sons.   Where his sons?

                        A sensual breeze.
                        A choking. The body
                        a smite.

//

            Achilles, deathless man void moonshine, I cut
my veins & see his name. His sons: rampant, melodic. Sweet

negotiations. *Love*
the violence that births you . Hate

the chirp of the birds you eat.
            Love me too, father. Love me.

After the Funeral

I prayed most nights for God to send my Grandfather back.
Prayer; an appeal for an intermediary service 'tween

> my gone-people & me, a parting of
> water. Sent petitions signed by myself 1000 times. Twice,

I remember knowing him again,
though he Dead. But what is Dead

> but to be without your worn juice?
> blood. I've been without before,

have you? Been withhhhhh
out that which keeps you? Alive,

> I know betrayal because my Grandma said,
> "He stopped visiting me in my dreams."

Her weeks had grown thin of him.
I burned my signatures, hoping he'd return

> to her, again. I'm sorry. I'm
> a liar. I begged God for another visit, even

after my heart plopped
out my mouth.

Prayer: bloodless, toothless. Despair,
drains the muscles.

> I wanted a father so bad any man would do.
> This does not apply to my grandfather. Though,

lineage is a container, *Grandpa* being
fatherfather. Prayer,

prayed & the still stayed still. Grandma
not gone, but I worry about her dreams.

She doesn't want to be *here* & without.
Could you stand sleeping with

one hand on the faint imprint of loss?
I reach far away from myself

to the water. The ship. The way away
from the first *from*. I ask God

for the first of the Lovelace line,
& call him away from another woman.

For Songs & Contests

I say *Anwar* & boys
relax their flexed fists. Anwar

taught me to throw hands before
I traced my name in clay.

Flat hand across the face is
power. Throw a punch if a nigga

gets dirty. & she did. Kicked my cousin
in the tender tendon, sent a shriek

out his mouth slicing
telephone wires.

I,

the only girl with hands,
knew my job. One jab

would not do—I learned
to hit in sequence. 1,2,3

& the blood kept leaving.
The watchers report on the brawl:

Clearly a God
was driving her .

"They May Become Wise."

—Genesis, King James Version, VIA TONI MORRISON

If I grow fruit in my backyard then I am a farmer. Everything I eat I sow.
I filter the water & spit seeds to the ground, watch grass make way
for a springing ripe.

Perhaps, I own my stomach. Perhaps,
every bite is a small me. Perhaps,
I am fertile in this way.

> A dog jumps the fence, I hose him back over; worms
> try to harvest home my apples—corral in the
> core—I spray a chili powder mix; but when snakes
> smoothen their body against my brown. Duck in &
> out the earth. We both know I cannot tender this
> death. This must be the shovel. Must be to the head.
> Long & vile for the slow burn that is a girl belly. All
> this till its eyes fatten to a plum's droop.

When there is no if:
I own the garden.
The boy is a thief his God
a snake. They crawl 'til
my middle is a burst persimmon.
My shovel's steel renders to rust
my dirt is named after another's son

everyone eats off the land.

Return to Sender

Daddy does the leaving but our browns
match. So we walk around the block & everyone knows
whose I am until he crosses the knotted gate
& the baseball field a swirling sand under
screeching wheels to never return.

send it up, send it through

Papa & I share a protruding forehead
& a love for vinyl, the coiled licorice I collect.
I am a direct translation
of his face, while Mama & I wander
aisle after aisle of vegetables grown
below a Dixon belt. Each passerby keen
to her pink-lipstick-&-pumps beauty.
No one sees our resemblance.

send it up, send it through

I think of Papa's leaving & imagine him
passing the porch lion I watch shake its plaster
& live out its open mouth roar
around his leg, but
my looks are still his.
This conjure does not crack the mirror.

send it up, send it through, send it right back to you

Roy Wilkins Recreational Center

The boys play "Ignition," & the girls dance
the only way 2003 allows—the bottom half

of my cornrows slapping my back. The thick braid
reminding me of what is mine & what is added.

Long hair because Alicia Keys has long hair
& I think she is the most beautiful girl &

I kissed her CD once before I fell asleep but right now
we are dancing & dancing to the words of Robert

who croons a deep thrum into the Rec center. The boys
are grabbing hands of the prettiest girls & in my case

the one with the fat ass. It is a birthday.
A celebration for 13 years of boyhood & R. Kelly

siphons. Walks the walls of this Queens party.
The boys' hands are trying to find the engine.

They are searching for what they claim to know,
but the girls know it's unknown.

As the hand slims along the seams of my red
shirt dress I think of what is unknown to me.

What it meant when Connie said Rod's penis is 9 inches long
& he showed everyone in the lunchroom to prove it.

All the girls who saw it, changed. I surprised by the ambition
of the unzip. How his face held no shame,

how the way the girls talked I thought they wanted to be
the penis rather than the hand. & Kels is still

the Pied Piper even in this room. As he inches
my seam & every girl sings every word.

For Songs & Contests

Achilles is in a foot race
against Memnon down
the block on 178th place.

All the girls & boys line up
on either side of Nikes.

One boy wrestles another down
to gravel by a handful of hair. *Loser
buys italian ices.*

The sun is pulsing at
the back of every neck by now.

(A girl shouts.)

*How your feet so fast
in them heavy ass boots?*

(Pop!) & both boys are on their feet.

If Achilles loses it's 'cause the street
tripped him.

(Someone divinity loathes is slumped
w/ an arrow in their back.)

Achilles lives his name,
but never gets the medal.

*now— while the gifts still wait—
whose trophy are you.
for some, gold fades.*

        The same ruin waits the coward

& the brave.

Ed

We reward the child for his bad deed by attaching a complex to his name & his father ends the year spurned under tire sipes. We let the boy walk,   watch the father make a dull grave.   Some   tear   up,   most murmur about the boy who can't take his eyes off his mother:

What shape the home a boy like that can grow in?   Size up the mother:

breast too ample   slit too high on the thigh.   *Maybe she seduced him?* Breastfeed when the sun lowers its head & even after the boy's lips hang over stubble.

Now he a grown man who want his mama. Mow the whole head off the man that made him.

Up the street they'd call Oedipus, Ed & say

something just ain't right   *he slept in the coop with the chickens too long.* Might even say

his Mama & him out doing the grown thing under the moonlight,   but eventually, everyone forgets every name, but the boy with the mischief night.

& no father gets a shield & no mother keeps a crown.

Moses II: The Lunchroom

Show me his blood/on you[1]
& the first spear is launched across
the cafeteria/a chocolate milk so high
it tap the fluorescent light
carton crashes down/linoleum now
a slide/everyone is throwing perfectly
good defrosted pizza/& perfectly good
fried apple bits an industrial bag names
tater-tots/one 7th grader laughs
his tots in the air/the ketchup
goes up & lands/on an air jordan
show me his blood /I'll point
you to the corner where edge
meets edge/& head
meets wall/that fist
parts the mouth
His God/ His God/ His God

[1] All quotes are from *Moses*, 1956 rendition. From Nefertari to Pharaoh, after the sea split and descended upon his men like a building folding in on itself.

Repurposing a Funeral

Cousin Anwar b-lines through J. Foster Phillips Funeral Home
& the petals around Grandpa's casket start to sweat.
He is here. Even though Grandpa pulled the knife—
told him he'd be just like his father. A man

who only loved his wife when he was not drunk.
Drove one hand on the steering wheel
the other wrapped around a cold Heineken.
He & the pale lager shared a brown bag

on nights when his irises were two times the size
of Aunty's engagement ring. When the moon hung
out the window like a plump belly his fists found
new addresses: his son's throat, his wife's chest, his daughter's door.

Anwar, a man with the hottest hands, receives an obituary
& the pages smoke. Meaning he spotted his niece's father.
The one who made his head a red creek. Broke a beer bottle
over it, & sprinted out the front door. *Like a bitch*, Anwar adds.

Left the new teeth sprawled all over the floor.
Someone reads a psalm. My Grandmother
wails like a leaving ship. A choir member heaves.
& where even are the gods?

& Anwar burns a hole in the obituary, but not
the 4x4 cardstock keepsake with Grandpa's face
he will wear above his chest every day after this.
                    One glance up,

he catches a smirk spreading across the face
like an unbuttoned blouse. His patent
leather shoes quicken to the assailant's side,
arms stretched long as a hearse. He gets close,

spouts *Nowhere to run now!*
                    & there go his hands, & all the heads stay bowed.

Exorcism

This is the white & green house.

This is my mother preparing the snacks for the preacher to bless the white & green house.

This is my uncle who lives in the basement of my mother's newly blessed white & green house.

This is my mother's car backing out the driveway behind the laundry basement my uncle lives in, in my mother's prayed over, creaky floored, white & green house.

This is my uncle jamming his stubby fingers inside the inner lip of my shorts & his mouth across my mouth when my mother peeled out the driveway, in the back of her church sanctified, squeaky wood, white & green house.

Practice

You are 7 & a mother

        in training. Your ankles swell

in empathy of your aunt's bowling ball

        figure beleaguered by the growing

unborn. She looks like she may tip

        over. You want her to,

you are a mother in training.

        At 9 the men in your family are nourished

by your hands. You can hold your niece

        without a curved back. At 12

your breasts brim above ground

        & you wonder if your milk

has curdled.

        It is all maternal: your concessions,

each private entering

        your private. The blood

that leaves you is not private, abdominal.

        Spit it on the sidewalk. Mother of

mothers, may I never shed another wall

        again.

Let Me Tell You a Thing

about desire. I walk my body
& know the inside of a man's
mouth before I can say the weather. Together
we make two subjects. He can be
any kind of cruelty, any kind
of treasure.

In another life

In China I am _____ as I am
in Tuscaloosa _____ as I am
in Queens _____ as I am
in Ghana _____ as I am
at 5 _____ as I am
at 9 _____ as I am
in the store _____ as I am
draped in silk, dragged in a box.

In another life

If a man calls me beautiful,
next I'm smoke. Lastly
I'm in the wind & unconsumable.
I know the way a door closes.
I see the hands brine my bones—
better than a body. No body.

In another life, I bet you were my _____.

Veterans Memorial Drive

I am not a woman
excited by war
relics, though
I am considering
buying a gun. The kind
lean as tenderloin, but still
burst the fire through. I mean,
I am a small girl
in her lonesome. No
guaranteed safety
of my nigga at night. No,
just me, & my sharpest knife
smoking an L
near the window sill;
there is an entire boulevard
for a veteran's memory
in Tuscaloosa.
Collective memory
is a hell of a snag.
My memory
is a long Uhaul
down Memorial Drive
disobeying traffic
I am the largest
on this paved liqueur
& even the smallest
child burnt does not
stop the maniacal laugh.
I wonder if this is history
when visiting a country
that has bombed you out
the wazoo. My God. Where
am I with my 12 gauge shotty? Who
am I but afraid
living in a country
that celebrates

a machine that kills
thousands of children
& also prints
God Bless America
on its license plates,
will garner me
the worst kind
of karma.

The "S" in *I Loves You, Porgy*

makes me think plurality. Maybe I can love you
with many selves. Or. I love all the *Porgys*.
Even as a colloquialism: a queering of
love as singular. English is a strange
language because *I loves*
& *He loves* are not
both grammarly. *I loves you,*
Porgy. Better to ask what man is not
Porgy.
The beauty of Nina's *Porgy* distorts
gravity. *Don't let him take me.*
The ceiling is in
the floor. There is one name
I cannot say.
Who is

—————

now—
beauty, a proposal on
refuse. Disposal.
Nina's eyes know
a fist too well. Not
well enough.
Pick one
out a
lineup.

Cyclops Girl Is a Good Host

Sometimes I invite a whole street
into my house. Boiling white rice.
Making curry chicken: what I
share of my mother I offer
all the neighbors. Even the boys
I am afraid will call me
nigger
in my own home.   I open my door to the boy I see   w/ my good eye
                           & then I can't   see.

The boy says
I have stabbed
your good eye.   I forgive,   say

                                       Come inside.

Blade twists.

                                       Come inside.

My eye doesn't heal.

                                       Come inside.

the boy:
point me to
my plate
of food.

He eats. I smile.

I hear him licking his fingers clean.

Letter to the Choking

Track the bone. As it enters
the body disguised as cheek
of Kingfish. How it lays in the
meat like it too would break
down at the enzyme. A sleek
pin ready to go down the long
pipe. Clog, poke, & prod the
pink inside. Lodged in what
is a fire exit. How quickly the
bone became a dam, a thick
tree trunk at the mouth of a
river.

You missed it. Because the
teeth were too busy being a
show, the tongue desperate
for a last taste swept the
gums for what was left of the
curry, & the throat, sweating
for something new to go
down, welcomed it.

You knew this would happen.
Your mama always says you
chew too quickly, don't even
let the food die in your mouth
before you swallow it. & now
the bone is here. Jammed
diagonal in the esophagus,
shortest distance to death.
Air can't come in or out, &
now you are a hot emergency.
Your whole body a pot with a
top that won't boil over. You
wrap your hands 'round your
throat to coax the budge.

Knees take turns rising. 30
seconds of the workout, the
body flopping to live, limbs
get tired, face drains. But the
bone is still there, so home
it has made marks in the
walls, & you vow to never let
another bone pass through
lips if you live.

Mr. & Me

Mr. & Me are   on all fours again   over the floor   like   some kind of
mountainous mammal   w/ so much splendor the sky   could end.   Here
   I am flayed.

      Later.   I am not opening & unsure why.   What rebukes his body?

Once. When I was 13 my Uncle put his hands—
                there was no blood
     though I wish there was
          a scar to say
this is where the story ended, or
     here is where I got his eyes.

Roan Beauty & Charger[1]

Anwar drove his mother's car like his was the only name
on the lease of the silver Dodge Charger

before he crashed it one night & the driver door caved
inward like the center of a spoon.

I'd never seen someone drive like they loved to fucking
drive. Turns so sharp the tires on one side

would tilt in the air. & I'd get scared. Inside or outside the
car. But Anwar spoke

to the steering wheel in a baritone, & this is how I learned
tenderness—watching him pull

the reins & stroke the car's silver mane. & under
the hood the horses beat their hooves

for him. Even when he traveled 53 miles past the gas light.
I think he even named that car

a woman's name. *Roan.* & he even believed her
when she said

she'd never leave him
on the battlefield.

[1] "Roan Beauty" & "Charger" are the names of Achilles's horses in *The Iliad*

Sharing Cake

I give you two slices of my aunty's
cake, my favorite cake in the world.
It is a pound cake she makes.
385° preheat, maybe.
I am not a baker, but I know
one slice makes me feel good.
Like the wooden finish
aunty's feet pace is not
where my back once laid.
Her son atop me, a knife
to my neck like the cutting board.

You told me that there are many
ways out. That our friendship
is a parked car, with the top down
& no safety lock. Once, you prayed
someone more *equipped*
would show for this job
& I wept like a shower head.

I did not think I was worthy
of the second slice. How delicious
my aunt makes the mundane. I
have never been a block
of clay, shapeless & seated, but
I was quiet & cooling when plucked
from the oven. & you eat
both slices of pound pastry
even when I asked you
to save one for your mother.
& we fake anger at the dining
table, in a room where the frames
don't rattle. 40s of Old English side
by side. We joke of a magic
our Americaness cannot excise. &
the fake fight bottoms out

to a fit of laughter because when I brought
two slices
I knew you'd eat both.

What I mean to say is
I am afraid that if I share you
you will leave.

Finally, Weep Freely

Pat lives atop Achilles's open chest in a thick
pendant, gaudy gold stones emblazon his face.
Achilles is an open weeper, & an angry drunk.
Pat died & the Gods lose the meaning of fickle.
Pat: the spur for the Olympic games. Pat's name is
on a two-finger ring across the hand of the
undying Heel. Pat's name is said 137 times outside
of my house as Achilles empties an entire case of
Old English in my garden waking all the
neighbors with his wilting. Everyone has to cry
for Pat. I don't envy Pat. I hate Achilles. I take him
home when he is beating his fists bloody at the
bar, his bile a whiskey distillery, screaming for the
DJ to play Maggot Brain. The nine minute
thirty-six second dirge by Funkadelic. The only
bellow comparable to his he says.

I envy the archive
of Pat.

I want
my grandfather
rendered in copper
at the entrance
of every state.

It is morning. Achilles is hunched over my toilet
with his R.I.P Pat tramp stamp. His only helmet
porcelain. Call him out:

I did not cry at my Grandfather's funeral
because someone told me I had to be strong,
but you were bestowed timeless grieving.
If the Gods authorized
an army's beheading
for your best friend,
then let's really do
vengeance.
Let's take up swords, rally
cars so big
they clog the I-20
here to Jersey.
I wanna cry,
I wanna rage,
& I want someone
to write about it .

Don't Pretty Me

Don't pretty me. Don't pretty me.

Don't pretty me. Don't pretty me.

Don't pretty me. Don't pretty me.

Don't pretty me. Don't pretty me.

Don't pretty me. Don't pretty me.

Don't pretty me. Don't pretty me.

Don't pretty me. Don't pretty me.

Don't pretty me. Don't pretty me.

Don't pretty me. Don't pretty me.

Don't pretty me. Don't pretty me.

Don't pretty me. Don't pretty me.

Don't pretty me. Don't pretty me.

Don't pretty me. Don't pretty me.

Don't pretty me. Don't pretty me.

Don't pretty me. Don't pretty me.

Don't pretty me. Don't pretty me.

Don't pretty me. Don't pretty me.

Don't pretty me. Don't pretty me.

Don't pretty me. Don't pretty me.

Don't.

Black Peter

Air is palatial & the apartment is boxy. (Bed is in the
kitchen. Grease pops from the chicken pan to the T.V.) He
& the squared windows stand, taut on teeth. The town a
green & brown checkerboard when he fly above it (above
it, the body indistinguishable from an oil slick). What a tall
mouth the projects are.

> Feet tingle the wood—
> bouncing blood.　　Air
> is a spacious coffin. Don't
> pay your body to the floor.
> Never land. Never land.
> Never land

Hourglass

A father exists, but not
much. How

        much is enough?
        Woodchuckers chuck

        & that's a sufficient riddle.
        There is a limit. Even when the action

is your name—*to father*
is a verb. Predictable

        that I ask about love. Lovelace
        my Grandfather's last

name, the first
of many branches on burned

        bark. I stand at the Black Warrior
        Dam & am alert at the lack

of alarm. I dip my toe in the town's
drinking water. I walk

        more than I drive, but once
        when I was high I curved into the right turn

of a casual street & thought
under the police car's siren

                a dead black boy lay over two solid
                yellow lines, & maybe it was a trip

        trapped in the blue note of a trombone.
        Dear God,

                    I hope so, or
                    I'm sliding every egg from my uterus. Give me

baron when the dead boys from the screen appear dead
everywhere.

                    Last week a wind
wandered into my car on the same street. It was

                    lost & non-threatening. I drove
                    it home, though we nearly passed

                                        its season.
It's Christmas

& Grandpa's empty
chair cracks my mother in half.   I rub

her face, he holds
my hand—sand

returning to sand.

When Your Vice Is a Man

A black & mild alone is my daddy leaving. The bud
of plastic recedes when it's still burning. The nub is ash.
Ashiness means I lack
coconut oil: *virgin only*—
contend with the politics of that. Now complicate:
my father thinks he's my father. I'm saying
ownership. I'm saying
my last name is leash-like. Now complicate: I wanted
the boy to leash me. A *bitch*. & here
I call him my first father
daddy.
I don't answer the phone for either. Call me a sickness.
Me & _____, old enough to father me, fuck
in a federal building.
I know how
to desecrate.
I'm scared. Complicate
used language: *up in flames*
goes a building
full of my fathers.

Roll Tide

Derrick Henry & I have similar-sized hands.
I know by way of immortality:
a cast of them in hardened cement,
a feature of the co-captain shrine
on the Tuscaloosa Quad.

My mama wants to know if I have seen him
IRL & my patience glints in its smallness.

This campus is big in its body, doubles
in density on game days.
Truthfully, I have aged out
of college campus recognition,

but mama insists on his unordinary:
to spot a 6'3", black man, 250 lbs is a possible
miracle.

& I will not say of his stature
a correlation to an inhuman body i.e. any non-bipedal
or feathered one. A someone,
someone could misplace w/ myth;

Henry . . . a durable guy.
The adjective "durable":
a cramped closet of tragic names,
the collapse of a body's height
under condensed lead.

Sen. John Tyler Morgan was a college sports fan
in his want of human bodies
to perform an unpaid labor.

Meaning, I have a relation
to the most tragic of names
that university buildings are named after.

& the stadium is dressed in Henry's
name every night:

A man who drove 357 miles
in a truck with two confederate flags as axles
chants Henry's name for the Heisman.
& I am in awe of how the field
spreads across a century.

I live in 2016, a year w/ lineage
beyond a goal post. & I cry
seeing Henry's hands forever in the ground.
Hands I've never seen, but through the TV screen.
& here even John Tyler Morgan must love the man w/ skin
he'd have once vouched to burn back to the earth.

I cheer w/ my mama for Henry winning the Heisman.
The game ends & the stadium is an emptying lake.
Blood rises when we win. It's tradition. Here's to the land
of game that lets a man reclaim the land. Raise glasses
& hope his mama good.

For the Days That Are Today

"it always seems a bit abstract doesn't it? Other people dying."
—PETER DINKLAGE AS TYRION LANNISTER, *Game of Thrones*

I want,
after waking to the news
that is always the news
& changing the Facebook
autoplay settings as to not
see the blood out
of where it is meant to be in
of the black / brown him / her / they,
to peer out my blinds
& see my left neighbor bundling
their shrub switches
into torch, my right neighbor's face
sobbing raw, my whole complex
making weapons of their outrage.

I want every person in the street.
I want every person in the street.
I want every person in this street.

I want their hands, not adorned
but useful in brass knuckles. Hands wielding
bats. Bike chains repurposed.
Hatchets. Hammers. Scythes & machetes.
I don't want guns in the street. This war
is personal (I prefer to feel
a tooth unhook
from gums). I want to see the white Alabama man
walking w/ me & we both
on the way together
for the black _____ murdered
again. I want every street
domestically in feet
en route to what would be

a star on the map of America.
Which could be DC / Baton Rouge /
NY / Minneapolis. I want
hands in lovers
hands walking. I want
children napping
in the arms
of their walking fathers.
The battle
is
this urgent. I want the blocks
thick w/ movement
'cause this
death
will not
be held.

Ruff Ryders Anthem

I'd cry if shame wore us

                  (WHAT)

outwinded from patriarchy

                  (WHAT)

my pussy draws crowds

                  (WHAT)

iced out   when the winter heatless

                  (WHAT)

we reap

                  (WHAT)

we

                  (WHAT)

thoroughbreds

                  (WHAT)

suitable scales for the salacious—

                  (WHAT)

call us something 'side our name

                  (WHAT)

find your spleen spanked

                  (WHAT)

you should know

                  (WHAT)

we've answered anger

                  (WHAT)

more times than we haven't

                  (WHAT)

pact of protection   (WHAT)   violence

                  (WHAT)

        (WHAT)

(WHAT)

an inheritance

For Songs & Contests

"Let him bow down to me! I am the greater king, / … the greater man."

—*THE ILIAD*

This is how
I shed the house:
one boy's broken
cheek after
another. I slapbox
& my hands
are the quickest.
Slapboxing,
the kind of fight
that does not
require reason.
Except. I want
a name. (Sound
familiar?) I
am in proximity
to named
men. In this way
I am any
daughter. Once
I knew a man
who fought
a river,
& kept
both hands. Once
I was called
Anwar's little
cousin.
Once, I didn't have
a name
at all. Who are you
if not boy
& brazen?

A heavy *thwack*
across a boy's face,
& I am first
of my
name.

"I Turned Myself Into Myself & Was Jesus"

—"Ego Tripping," NIKKI GIOVANNI

My bones converge to altar / bloated
in bad breathing habits / Bus

a table w/ me, Commandment 1 / Know
the way I shake wool / Get my hair braided

& spend 4 hours in the hands
of another black woman / wrapping each hair round

the other / cause my crown immaculate / while
a man prayed to me / quivering in need

of my looking / divine on a cross / My head
thornfull / 'Til

a wolf handed
me his whole fur / I handed him

off my head / my hair / I think
that's what Daddy meant / by reciprocity

an inconvenience of need / that leads me
back to me / I don't make the rules I am / Once

the deed / in need of repentance / was done
My funeral was

casket open / Buried
mouth open / gold fronts gaping

as to not mistake / the gates of heaven
the only way in / through me

Citizenship

I am afraid

of what I mean   by loyalty.

A down   ass   bitch.

I'd ride to the grave for love

                    but what of where   I made country

of the place I live   my possible death plot?

I wring my birth certificate of

            what will bury me in due time.

                    What will come to the door

asking of my allegiance?

In times of war I lack metaphor.
War can be defined as

                            everyone fucking up my money,

                            institutions & individuals alike.

If I love you

                    I have threatened someone in your name.

            I'm from America, blame my blood   for the coming blood.

            Blame my murder & assault   on someone's   tame renaming.

& still am I even *from* here?

Would I make myself violent   in the name of a nation?

Yes,

I would kill for my mother.

Still, I Don't Love My Father

In a Greyhound Station his last name
is read before my first

by the entrance attendant I hand my ticket to. Who
is kind & asks me "Why didn't you bring

me breakfast?" *It is 4 in the morning*, I blush
to myself.   Oedipus, I do not *want*

the older stranger inquiring
on his day's first meal. I respond, "You

were bringing me breakfast today," a snappy
teen in my gullet. Glum, but glinting

in my cheekiness extended
to the aged stranger who I knew

was Nigerian before his exhort of such. I don't love
my father, but the Greyhound says, "Your name

is beautiful is it African?" & he means
my name,
not
my last.

& I cannot say I believe in love because
I love my father. No. That country stretched

itself large w/ new children. There is no room.
But I believe in love, 20th of January, even

in a Greyhound bus station where
fluorescents blink to bleakness, even

as my home country inchoate
itches to slide me off its flag,

when I remember the Attendant in Atlanta
taught me hello in Ibo

when I told him I could not speak
my father's language. Oh,

how the weeping followed.

Ugly

I tell you. Chipped my tooth
on a pork chop bone,

most of my hair on my legs,
baldheaded,

            4headed,
headed

a woman.
I scarred my left foot in new heels.

At worst
I'm a sad nigga.

Tarbabe culpable,
steal your son. *u - g - l - y*

I be my uglyass, alibi-less,
self & your father still crawls

through my window.
Ugz

    Magee.
my ass fat & I know

who wants it fatter:
    you

plump
& phallic applause:

Penal insistence prescribes me pretty,
I told you what I am & you Presidented

your ego, baby—I dying is
Nationbuilding,

I

    (*womanwomanwoman*
        womanwomanwoman
           womanwomanwoman)(*black*)

plump &   You
          [chantchantchant]

   witch :: *witch* :: *witch*
& I'm in a skewer the long ways

sluggish above an inferno.
nationbuilding,

make mess of me—
the first holiday roast.

I'm on
fire [for you baby].

What's new? What's the weather?
Singed to the bone

like a hate crime
it's nationbuilding

burning me (*woman*)(*black*) =
Doorknobdead.

My teeth starch straight
knowing you is the same without

me:
deadasdeadasdead

I know what I
know. Here's a secret

I ain't dying, baby—
I'm black &

ugly as
ever Alive.

On Knowing

That I, too, come from the lineage & loins
of Achilles. That I see the man, be him
named Daniel, & urge the machete
across the width of him. Just so.
A tree chop.
To know that his crying face
is an Achilles I come from
too
makes me fear my own name. Newlyconvicted-
crying-serial-rapist
will not leave my computer screen. His mouth
stretched like it's tearing away from its own teeth. &.
Still there are other men. Other
Daniels. Maybe
one will handcraft my favorite Chai today. &
maybe he will even outstretch
the doors of some Starbucks on a street
filled with other impossible faces, for me. &. Maybe
Daniel & I will share a smile
& that will be the sky's reprieve. Never knowing
that that man too is a Daniel.
Even the fictional have the power to speak
& make me guess where my fists are. Truth:
I, at all times, am the smallest parts of me: my ears,
so tiny I often wonder how they hear at all,
a nose, that can wiggle left & right & barely
traverse the face. Too, my hands, the things that want
to rip the reddening skin of the crying ex-officer
Daniel, can parse
a coiled curl & unmap the locks of a knot, but
I see Daniel—envision a shield fashioned
for me by a God— I see so many black girls.
Consider me. Consider me. Envisioning
the attacker again. What it means to be a fighter,
who did not fight
for her own body.

What else speaks better than
the pooling of blood? What else
is my greatest fear, but that I too
am capable of this carnage?
That a God
too
will still love me.

Untitled

Your Neighbor's Ex-Boyfriend says he'd pay
to see *that*. Referring to your previous admission to lay

hands on Caroline-Across-The-Way's Husband
if he blackened her eye or so much as a yelp

for help extended from her mouth.
You say you'd fight, but inside you promise

rain. Of blood. Of blows. You are
the second coming of your limbs when

the circulation can't slow. Enraged.
The list is long with men you want

to excise. Your Aunt's Ex-Husband.
Terrell from the 5th Grade. That one

Uncle. & here, a 47 looking, 35
year old white man offers

to patron your bludgeon of a stand-in
for the long list. All of the men

from the past & each tooth you
can pluck right up from their gums. This

is an offer you cannot refuse. White
men of the world filling your pocket

with big bills to watch you
blotch the skin where it was smooth.

& what an enticing trap,
money.

                              Violence
will drive you off a steep

staircase on wobbly wheels. You know
the way it bloats your muscles. But,

Caroline's husband is
the scum that which other scum

eats its dinner off & her 17-year-old
son says he's afraid. He will hit

her again. Tonight. A lush plead: *please,
don't leave*. & you want to solve this

with the one solution you know.
Blood.

Blood.
Blood.

                    Instead, you are swilled
with swigs of beer. You are no

hero. Your mouth
a mulch of butterscotch. Who

do you hold your fists back for?
                                        You

have recurring nightmares where
there is a man holding you

underwater. He wants to take—
& you cannot land a punch

not a scratch. Much the way
you exit Caroline's house,

her husband & sons behind you.
Your name, Nabila,

means noble. The door closes behind you,
where is your name now?

Notes

"For Songs & Contest" (1) quotes Homer's *The Iliad*, book 24.201: "Clearly a God was driving him."

"They May Become Wise" takes its name from the Angela Davis & Toni Morrison talk "Literacy, Libraries, & Liberation," which is an adaptation of a quote from the book of Genesis in the Bible.

"Return to Sender" is after the poet Yolanda Franklin. The poem works in the tradition of Michael Afaa Weaver's form The Bop & borrows the line "send it up, send it through" from D'Angelo's "Send it On" as the form's refrain.

"For Songs & Contest" (2) quotes Homer's *The Iliad*, book 9.385-387: "the same honor waits / for the coward and the brave."

"Exorcism" is after *Visiting St. Elizabeth's* by Elizabeth Bishop.

"Let Me Tell You a Thing" borrows the line "In another life I bet you were my" from D'Angelo's "Another Life" in *Black Messiah*, & works in the tradition of Michael Afaa Weaver's poetic form The Bop.

"Veterans Memorial Drive" references the major intersection in Tuscaloosa, AL which memorializes veterans through a display featuring a faux tank & helicopter.

"The "S" in *I Loves You, Porgy*" references & quotes Nina Simone's performance of "I Loves You, Porgy" off of her 1958 release *Little Girl Blue*.

Roan Beauty & *Charger* takes its title from the names of Achilles's horses in *The Iliad*.

"Sharing Cake" was written for my sister & best friend Thiahera Nurse & refers to my late Aunt Patricia Burris's pound cake, the greatest in the world.

"Black Peter" is partly inspired by & quotes *Peter Pan*.

"Roll Tide" is for Derrick Henry & my Mama & quotes a sportscaster from *The Bleacher Report* video 11.28.2015: "*Henry . . . a durable guy.*"

"For the Days That Are Today" features an epigraph from *Game of Thrones* character Tyrion Lannister.

"Ruff Ryders Anthem" takes its title & repeated "(WHAT)" from the DMX song "Ruff Ryders Anthem" produced by Swizz Beatz. In the *Complex* article "Swizz Beatz Tells All: The Stories Behind His Classic Records" Swizz Beatz explains that DMX did not actually want to record the record because he thought the beat was too Rock 'n' Roll. He then goes on to expound upon the process of encouragement & trust between him & X, "The 'What!' ad-lib and all of that came about in the middle of us hyping him up. We left it in the track to add energy. Collectively, we came up with that vibe. It was his best shit at that time. Since then, X has trusted my judgment."

"For Songs & Contest (3)" features an epigraph from *The Iliad*, book 9.192: "Let him bow down to me! I am the greater king/I am the elder-born, I claim—the greater man."

"I Turned Myself Into Myself & Was Jesus" borrows its title from Nikki Giovanni's poem "Ego Tripping" from her collection entitled *My House*.

"Ugly" quotes the cheerleader cheer & overall youth rhyme "Ugly": "U-G-L-Y you ain't got no alibi / you ugly / yeah yeah / you ugly" & also quotes The Notorious B.I.G's "One More Chance" from *Ready to Die*: "heart throb never, Black and ugly as ever."

"On Knowing" is inspired by Aracelis Girmay's *On Kindness*. & thinks of/considers S.H., T.B., C.R., F., R.C., R.G., T.M., S.B., S.E., C.J., K. June, A. June, J. June, the 13 women who testified against ex-officer & rapist Daniel Holtzclaw.

Acknowledgments & Gratitude

Gratitude to the editors of the following publications who believed in, sometimes varying versions of, my poems & published them:

The Adroit Journal: "Sons of Achilles" & "'I Turned Myself Into Myself & Was Jesus'"
BOAAT Journal: "Roan Beauty & Charger"
The Breakbeat Poets: Black Girl Magic: "For Songs & Contest (3)"
Day One: "Roy Wilkins Recreational Center"
Diagram: "Cyclops Girl Is a Good Host"
ESPNW: "Roll Tide"
Iron Horse Review: "Citizenship"
Lineage of Mirrors (Winter Tangerine): "The Preamble," "Ruff Ryders," & "Ugly"
Muzzle Magazine: "When Your Vice Is a Man"
The Offing Magazine: "Veterans Memorial Drive"
Poetry Witch Magazine: "Return to Sender"
The Southeast Review: "Hourglass"
Vinyl: "For the Days That Are Today"

Gratitude to the late great Tamara Natalie Madden, whose work & brilliance I am forever grateful for. May you be resting well.

Gratitudes to the Fam:

Thank God, divine timing, the ancestors, & my Mama (Mama I love you so much, you were the first to introduce me to language. Spent time reading with me when you were working a full-time job. I can't thank you enough for what you've done for me). & my Granny Sylvia. & my Pops. & my whole fam.

RIP Grandpa, RIP Aunty Pat, RIP Mr. Goldman who put *Song of Solomon* in my hands my junior year in High School, RIP Stephanie, Dominic, + Amegie all gone too soon.

First of all I wanna thank my connect. Thiahera: my sisterSHIP, our youngest selves would be proud of who we are becoming. Jayson: what a beacon you stay. Paula: Twin, we walk side by side foreva, eva. Ghost Crew: may we be nowhere & everywhere.

To my partners in rigor, thank you for pushing my imagination, my craft, my mind & my heart. I am forever changed because of our bonds, thankful to be writing alongside y'all until the end:

Thiahera, Jayson, Paul, Ish, Blue, Christian, Ashley B., Ashley V., Sydney, Sean B., Charleen, Justin, Taylor, Jeremy, Jerriod, Desiree, Cortney, Monica, Sarah B., Emma, Jovonna, Troizel, Sammie, Hugh, Shiyah, James, Tafisha, Jonah, Diamond, Ebony, Najee, Clint, Yolanda, McKindy, Jessica, Jennifer, Aurora, Shaelyn, Kayleb, Connor, Kit, David, Jeremiah, Darian, Elizabeth R., Nisha, All my Bama Fam, Tommy, Leah, Julian, Ty, Nadia, Whole Trill Fam, Fall '15 Classics Workshop,

The Big Homies: Derrick + Kiese,

Both of The Conversation Literary Festival cycles Fellows + Staff, '16 in no particular order: Jayson / Paul / Cortney / Angel / Safia / Mega (BIG UP THE SELECTOR) / Hanif / Elizabeth / Danez / Desiree / Ishmael / Jeremy / Jerriod / Nate / José / Aziza // '17 in no particular order: Taylor / Charleen / Marwa / Paul / Gabriel / Raven / Safia / Hieu / Fatima / Jonah / Hanif / Jayson / Monica / Justin / Tafisha / Xandria / Nicholas / Ashley / Luther / Francis / Sean / Ishmael,

Urban Word & my first teachers Willie, Ajay, Ish, Thia, Blue, Christian, Sean B., Aracelis, Patrick, Mikal, Mahogany, & Jon you all were my first examples of what it could look like to be a healthy writer invested in community, peer mentorship, & teaching.

The Weavers Fellowship, Khalif, Solo, Cool, the whole Callaloo Creative Writers Workshop cohort (2015), Tin House cohort 2016, *Letters to the Future* cohort (2014), & *Writing Across Cultures* cohort (2015), I am thankful to have learned from you. What a blessing it is to be supported & cared for by y'all. We got us.

For my ATL Fam, who beared with the poems I wrote before I read any books. Your support made my dream feel tangible, thank you: Kam, Faith, Aaris, Marvito, Megan, Katherine (BOMB Radio foreva!), Heidi, Priyanka, Karen G, & CUPSI teams '11, '12, & '13.

I am in deep & infinite gratitude to my teachers & mentors who saw my work & met me with generosity: Dr. Nagueyalti Warren, Mahogany Browne, Erica Hunt, Rigoberto González, Nicole Sealy, Gregory Pardlo, Vievee Francis, Ravi Howard, Joel Brower, Jericho Brown, & L. Lamar Wilson. You opened up a new world for me, thank you. & to the institutions that fueled this endeavor through time, study, &/or funds thank you: Cave Canem, Callaloo, Tin House & UA Tuscaloosa.

An entire small ships worth of gratitude to KMA & the whole YesYes Books family. Your belief in this project, beginning from its chapbook draft, has been an incredible blessing. I cannot thank you enough for urging me forward.

Finally. Thank you, reader. Thank you for taking this journey in words with me. I am in awe, honored, & humbled by the idea of someone beyond myself reading these poems. Thank you for taking the time.

NABILA LOVELACE is a born & raised Queens native, as well as a first-generation American. Her parents hail from Trinidad & Tobago & Nigeria. *Sons of Achilles*, her debut book of poems, was released by YesYes Books in early 2018. Currently you can find her kicking it in Tuscaloosa.

Also from YesYes Books

FULL-LENGTH COLLECTIONS

i be, but i ain't by Aziza Barnes
The Feeder by Jennifer Jackson Berry
What Runs Over by Kayleb Rae Candrilli
Love the Stranger by Jay Deshpande
Blues Triumphant by Jonterri Gadson
North of Order by Nicholas Gulig
Meet Me Here at Dawn by Sophie Klahr
I Don't Mind If You're Feeling Alone by Thomas Patrick Levy
If I Should Say I Have Hope by Lynn Melnick
Landscape with Sex and Violence by Lynn Melnick
Good Morning America I Am Hungry and On Fire by jamie mortara
some planet by jamie mortara
Boyishly by Tanya Olson
Pelican by Emily O'Neill
The Youngest Butcher in Illinois by Robert Ostrom
A New Language for Falling Out of Love by Meghan Privitello
I'm So Fine: A List of Famous Men & What I Had On by Khadijah Queen
American Barricade by Danniel Schoonebeek
The Anatomist by Taryn Schwilling
Gilt by Raena Shirali
Panic Attack, USA by Nate Slawson
[insert] boy by Danez Smith
Man vs Sky by Corey Zeller
The Bones of Us by J. Bradley
　　[Art by Adam Scott Mazer]

CHAPBOOK COLLECTIONS

VINYL 45S
After by Fatimah Asghar
Inside My Electric City by Caylin Capra-Thomas
Dream with a Glass Chamber by Aricka Foreman
Pepper Girl by Jonterri Gadson
Of Darkness and Tumbling by Mónica Gomery

Bad Star by Rebecca Hazelton
Makeshift Cathedral by Peter LaBerge
Still, the Shore by Keith Leonard
Please Don't Leave Me Scarlett Johansson by Thomas Patrick Levy
Juned by Jenn Marie Nunes
A History of Flamboyance by Justin Phillip Reed
No by Ocean Vuong
This American Ghost by Michael Wasson

BLUE NOTE EDITIONS
Beastgirl & Other Origin Myths by Elizabeth Acevedo
Kissing Caskets by Mahogany L. Browne
One Above One Below: Positions & Lamentations by Gala Mukomolova

COMPANION SERIES
Inadequate Grave by Brandon Courtney
The Rest of the Body by Jay Deshpande